ABC
ZOO

ILLUSTRATED BY
CONSTANCE BEAUGEARD

Plurus BOOKS
© 2014
An Imprint of Wimbledon Publishing Company Limited
75-76 Blackfriars Road, London SE1 8HA

For Jess, Noah & Beau.
May you never stop exploring the world,
And the wonderful things it holds as you grow up.

Aa

Bb

Buffalo

Buffel

Büffel

Bufalo

Búfalo

Cc

🇬🇧 Chameleon

🇫🇷 Caméléon

🇩🇪 Chamäleon

🇮🇹 Camaleonte

🇪🇸 Camaleón

Dolphin

Dauphin

Delfin

Delfino

Delfín

Dd

Elephant

Eléphant

Elefant

Elefante

Elefante

Flamingo
Flamant
Flamingo
Fenicottero
Flamenco

Ff

Gg

H h

Hippopotamus

Hippopotame

Nilpferd

Ippopotamo

Hipopótamo

Ii

JESS

🇬🇧 Ibis

🇫🇷 Ibis

🇩🇪 Ibis

🇮🇹 Ibis

🇪🇸 Ibis

🇬🇧	Jaguar
🇫🇷	Jaguar
🇩🇪	Jaguar
🇮🇪	Giaguaro
🇪🇸	Jaguar

Jj

Kk

Lion

Lion

Löwe

Leone

León

L l

Mm

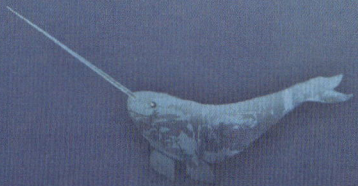

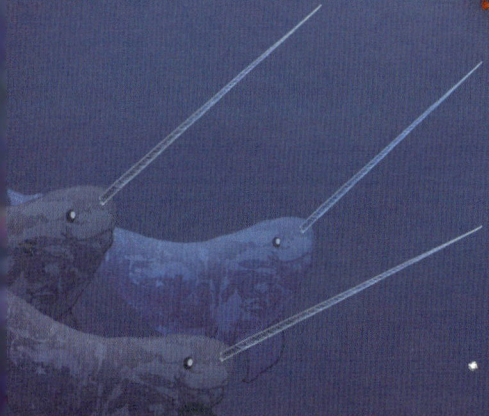

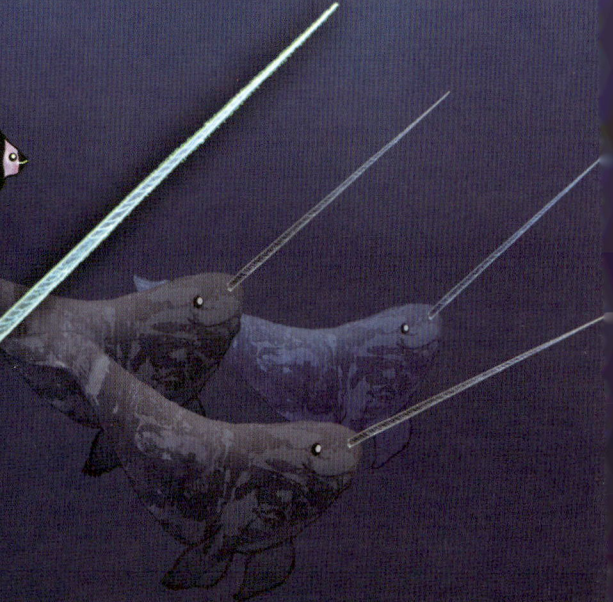

🇬🇧 Narwhal

🇫🇷 Narwhal

🇩🇪 Narwhal

🇮🇪 Narvalo

🇪🇸 Narval

Nn

Oo

Peacock

Paon

Pfau

Pavone

Pavo Real

Pp

Qq

Reindeer

Renne

Ren

Renna

Reno

S s

Toucan

Toucan

Tukan

Tucano

Tucán

T t

Uu

Vv

Vulpes Pallida

Vulpes Pallida

Vulpes Pallida

Vulpes Pallida

Vulpes Pallida

Ww

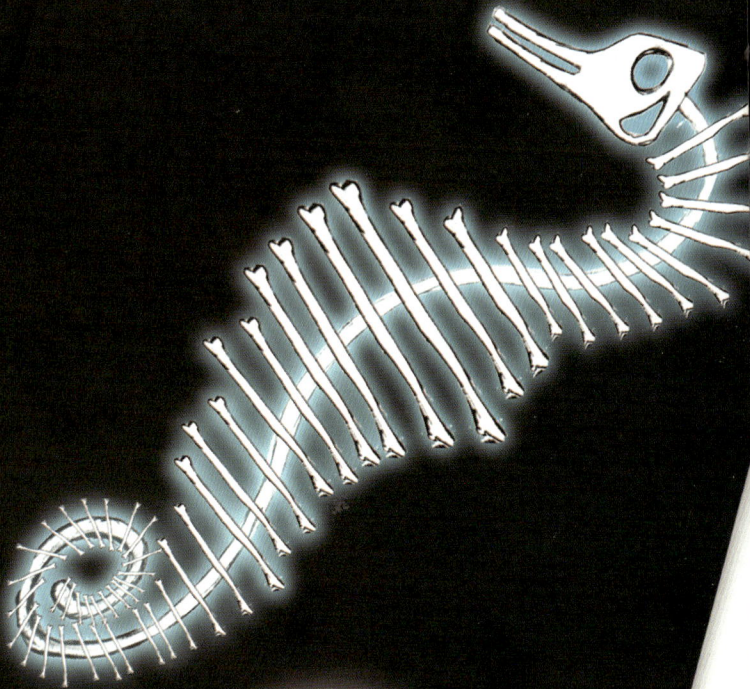

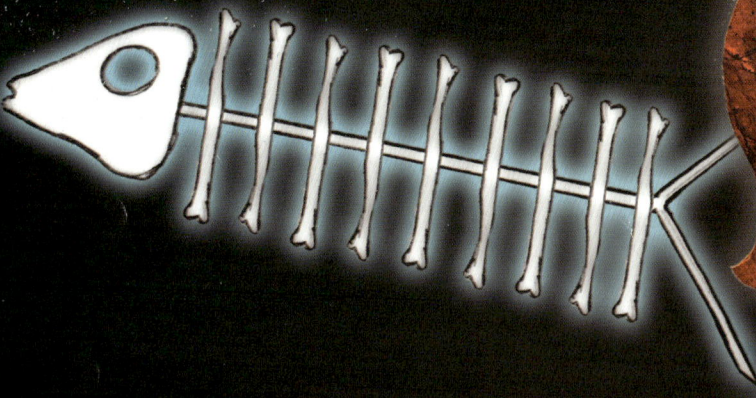

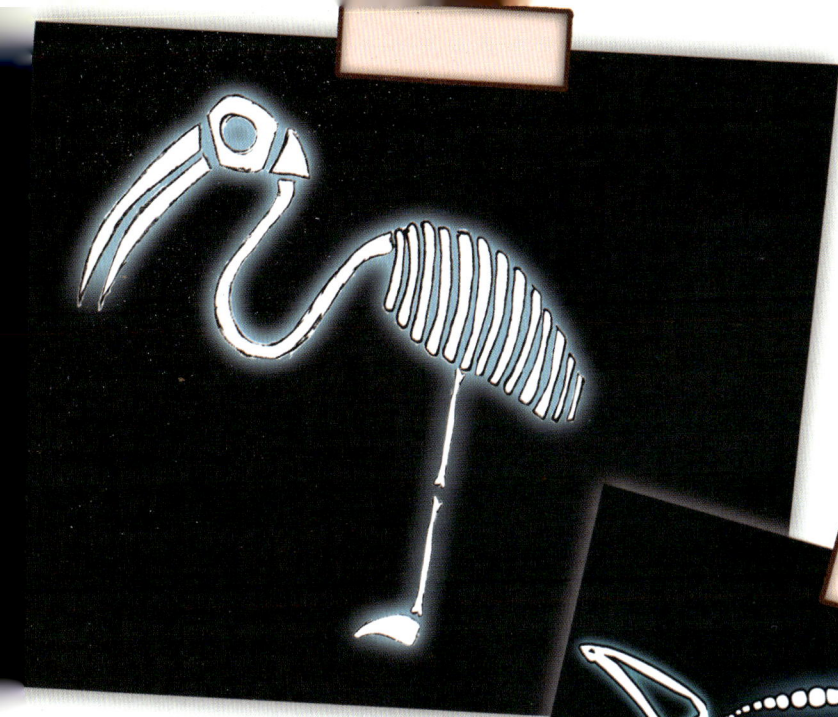

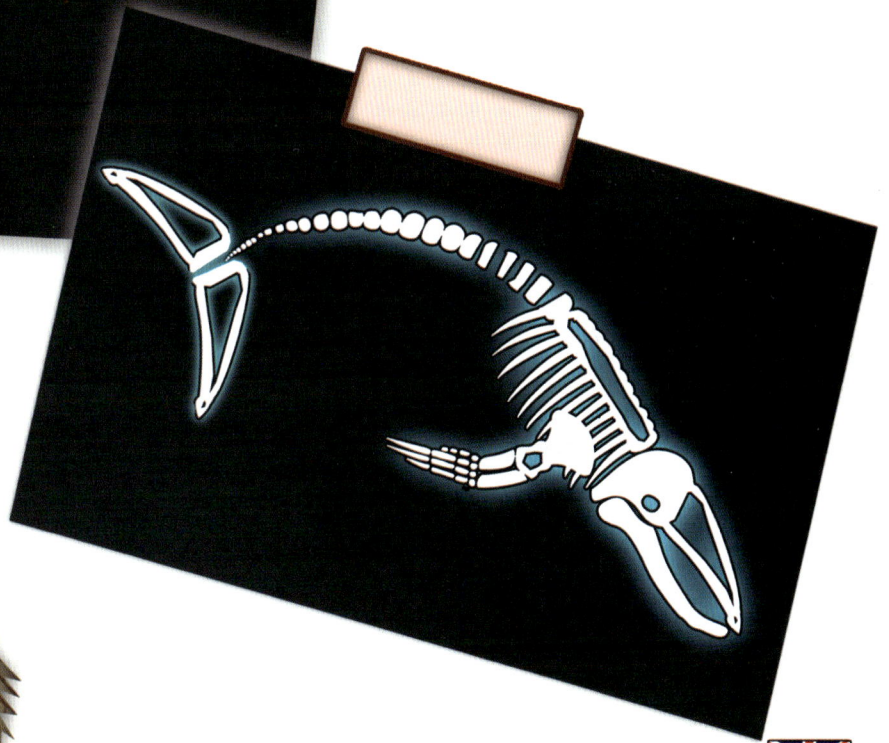

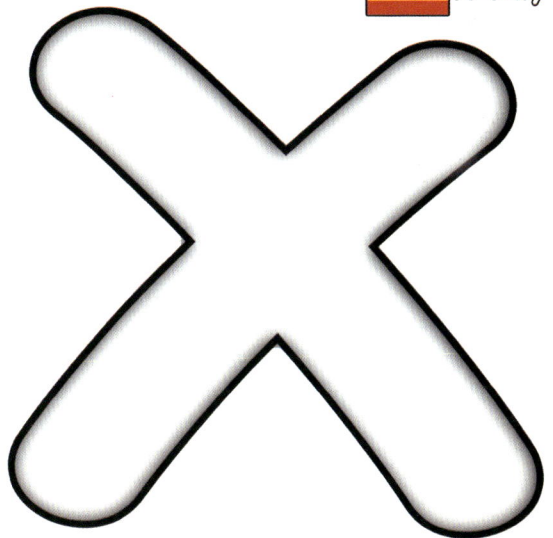

Yy

Z

ZO

NOAH

BEAU

ZOO